GETTING PAID TO
Moderate
Websites

CARLA MOONEY

ROSEN
PUBLISHING®

New York

Published in 2017 by The Rosen Publishing Group, Inc.
29 East 21st Street, New York, NY 10010

Library of Congress Cataloging-in-Publication Data

Names: Mooney, Carla, author.
Title: Getting paid to moderate websites / Carla Mooney.
Description: New York : Rosen Publishing, 2017. | Series.
  Turning your tech hobbies into a career | Includes index.
Identifiers: ISBN 9781508173007 (library bound)
Subjects: LCSH: Web sites—Juvenile literature. | Computer industry—Vocational guidance—Juvenile literature. | Computer industry—Customer services—Juvenile literature. | Computer technical support—Juvenile literature.
Classification: LCC TK5105.888 M656 2017 | DDC 004.67023—dc23

Manufactured in Malaysia

Contents

Introduction

Working from her home in southwest London, Dawn Kitchener sits in front of her laptop reading an animated bulletin board discussion about dangerous dogs. The back and forth among the online posters is quickly getting heated. In a February 2012 article for the *Guardian*, one poster responds to another, typing, "Michelle you are speaking a load of cr*p excuse the language!! I have a staff and she is the most lovable dog I know! By suggesting staffies need to be seized will only heighten illegal dog breeding ... Grow up woman, and think about what you write!" Kitchener's laptop chimes as more people add comments to the online conversation. For the moment, Kitchener watches the online conversation develop on the website of a British morning television show. Before long, she will get involved in the thread's discussion.

Kitchener works for a company called eModeration as a website moderator. The website's owner is one of her clients. Instead of posting her own thoughts on the topic, Kitchener's job is to sanitize internet discussion threads. She moderates discussions on a variety of topics, from dogs to car dealerships to current affairs. Some of what Kitchener does as a moderator involves intercepting comments on internet message boards and forums before they can be seen publicly, a practice that is becoming more common among online forums. "The nub of

A website moderator works while enjoying a cup of coffee at a local coffee house. With a laptop and internet access, she can review forum comments from anywhere.

what I'm doing is making sure nothing libelous is said or illegal is posted," she explains in a February 2012 interview with the *Guardian*.

Today, comments go onto message boards instantly. Kitchener's job is to remove anything offensive as quickly as possible. Her laptop gives her a special moderator's view of the comments. It highlights sensitive words, such as any profanity or any drug-related words in red. Anything flagged questionable gets reviewed and, if necessary, removed immediately. "This one that says 'cr*p,' I know I'll just delete that straight away," she explains.

Most of the time, Kitchener spends her time deleting minor offenses. Sometimes, online conversations can get intense. "It really depends on the news," she says. "If something happens and gets featured on the programme, you might get lots of racist comments coming in, for example." Sometimes, some of the most provocative topics have no connection to current events, but rather someone boasting, causing others to jump into the conversation.

In addition to removing offensive posts, Kitchener notifies the website provider if further investigation of a poster may be needed. In some cases, posters who frequently make abusive or offensive comments are warned or even barred from the site. However, Kitchener says that banning does little to stop someone who is determined to keep posting on a site. "The problem with the Internet is if you're banned, you can just re-create another user identity," she says. "That's why you constantly have to keep on top of it."

Although she works alone at home, Kitchener is connected to eModeration's other home-based workers. From anywhere in the world, the coworkers chat through instant messaging,

Skype, email, and a virtual office called Campfire. Online, the workers interact and support each other, like those in a regular office environment.

For people who like to get involved online, a job working as a website moderator could be a good one. They can take the tech skills and online savvy they have learned from participating in online communities and social media and turn these skills into a career as a website moderator.

Chapter ONE

Moderating Websites

Since the launch of the World Wide Web in 1991, the internet has quickly become an integral part of life for people around the world. In its early years, the internet was primarily a source of information, a resource people could use to find out addresses, company history, or news. In the early 2000s, the way in which people used the internet began to change. Users began to create and upload their own content, posting writing, pictures, video, and music. They could invite others to view and comment on their content. They created and added to the information online.

Today, many websites, games, social apps, and online stores have active user communities. Users post comments and questions on message boards or use chat services to interact with other users and contact customer service. Most websites

Former President Bill Clinton and Vice President Al Gore wire the ceiling with communication wire as part of Net Day 1996, an effort to get school classrooms connected to the Internet.

that have message boards, chat rooms, or allow users to post comments also have terms of service that define what is acceptable vs. unacceptable behavior on the site. Unacceptable behavior often includes posts that have links to illegal downloads or pornography and posts that attack other users or disrupt the online conversation. Unacceptable posts also include those that contain vulgar or profane language, drug references, bigotry, or other offensive language.

Unacceptable posts that violate the website's terms of service must be deleted, a job that falls to website moderators. Website moderators stay behind the scenes of online communities, helping users resolve issues safely and policing offensive and unacceptable posts. They are special users who have the authority to edit or delete other users' posts. An effective moderator has a good working knowledge of the site's terms of service in order to identify unacceptable posts. He or she must also be able to enforce the rules fairly, regardless of personal opinions on an issue.

WHAT DOES A MODERATOR DO?

Sometimes called community moderators or online content moderators, website moderators monitor all of the places users can upload comments and posts on company websites, including the websites of news and entertainment organizations. Every day, they oversee social media platforms, forums, blogs, and other online communities. They search for and identify unacceptable posts and remove them from the sites as needed.

In addition to scanning for inappropriate posts, moderators often work to engage users in online communities. They encourage others to participate in online discussions and keep discussions on topic. When discussions begin to veer off topic, moderators redirect the users back to the site's topic. Moderators also respond to member comments and move them into the proper categories on a message board as needed. They answer emails from members and address complaints offline to resolve any problems. When disputes arise between members, moderators step in to defuse the situation. Some moderators engage in search engine marketing, which improves the ability of people to search for and find the site. Others use software tools to analyze site metrics. For example, they might measure and report on the popularity or the number of views for a post or trending topic in the forum.

Kathleen Lewis is a website moderator for a gardening site. In an article for ewomanweb.com, she describes a typical day on the job, saying, "Overlooking my snow-covered garden, I casually open my laptop and begin my day. As I scan through my favorite gardening website, I am slapped in the face with comments that have nothing to do with gardening—some vile and repulsive and some just plain off-topic. One-by-one, I [as] an online content moderator of that gardening site, delete the comments and remind the offenders the rules of the forums. On the rare occasion, when a repeat offender just won't give up, I add their name and URL to the block list. When it comes to cleaning up the nastiness, it's my job to make sure the offenders are sent off to some other space within the wonderful world of the web." For moderators like Lewis, the main responsibility of the job is to protect a company's brand and image by monitoring and moderating its online sites.

GROWING NEED FOR MODERATORS

Online message boards or forums are places where people gather online to discuss various topics. In these forums, users can ask questions and post comments. Many companies and websites use online message forums as a tool to bring people to their sites, as the changing content of forums keeps people returning. There are forums for almost every topic imaginable, from playing Irish music to body piercing to world politics. Some forums are open to the public and allow anyone to post comments, while others require invitations from members.

As websites, chat rooms, and community forums have exploded all over the internet, the demand for community moderators has also grown. Nearly all active message forums need some sort of moderation, as anyone can post just about anything they want online. If left unmoderated, a forum or message board can quickly fill with off-topic, inappropriate, and even illegal activity. To protect themselves from any legal liability, website owners want to remove any posts that contain or support illegal activity, such as comments that communicate about selling black market drugs or guns. Site owners also want to make sure that their boards remain on topic.

Moderators also keep conversations among members from escalating into hostile arguments. Many message boards contain flaming and trolling posts. Flaming is the online term for yelling at another user. Trolling occurs when a user posts a comment just to be annoying or to deliberately cause other users to get upset. Moderators step in to remove these posts, calm users, and resolve issues.

Small businesses and website hosts quickly discover that as the activity increases on their sites, they need constant

A mother supervises her daughter as she uses her laptop to go on the internet. Similarly, companies need website moderators to supervise websites, forums, and chat rooms.

supervision. Many companies and hosts do not have the capability to moderate the sites themselves, so they turn to either filtering software or moderators to censor the content on their sites. Filtering software works by identifying and filtering specific words and phrases that the site's webmaster marks as offensive. While filtering software can work well for removing foul language, it often falls short on censoring more complex content. In these cases, hiring moderators who skim through discussions and message boards looking for inappropriate and off-topic content is often a better approach.

Sometimes, even moderators can fail to identify inappropriate content in a timely manner. Moderators are human, and they cannot always be online moderating every user comment. Being away from the job for a few hours, or even a few minutes, can lead to a flurry of comments that quickly escalates into offensive or off-topic posts.

CONTENT MODERATION

A specialized area of website moderation, called content moderation, has also grown in recent years. Content moderators remove offensive material from social networking sites and other websites. As social media has become more popular, it has also attracted its share of inappropriate content, from pornographic images to terrorist videos. Social media sites rely on content moderators to find and remove offensive, and sometimes gruesome content, before users see it. Hemanshu Nigam, chief executive officer of SSP Blue, an online safety consulting company, estimates that there are well over 100,000 content moderators working to clean up social media sites, mobile apps, and cloud storage services worldwide. Much of the work is done in secret, with many tech companies making moderators sign strict nondisclosure agreements that prohibit them from talking about their work. "The job they're doing is basically screening content that's posted to social media or cloud storage, and just making sure that whatever is posted fits the standards of the company that is running the service. They're really kind of the police of the Internet, and this requires seeing thousands and thousands of images and robotically going through this checklist to make sure they fit with the [company's] guidelines," said Adrian Chen, a reporter who researched and reported on content

Job Hazards

A job as a website moderator has several benefits, including the ability to work from home and have flexible hours. At the same time, there are some downsides to this type of work. First, moderators frequently have to deal with unpleasant and difficult people. They must remain patient and keep their emotions under control, even when difficult users direct hateful and abusive comments at them. In addition, some moderators find it difficult to hide their own feelings on sensitive topics, like politics or human rights. Also, the moderator's privacy is not guaranteed. Users who dislike the moderator and his or her policies could attempt to hack into his or her personal information. Several moderators at Reddit's many online communities have reported regularly receiving hate mail and death threats.

For content moderators who are frequently exposed to graphic pictures and videos, the job can also take a psychological toll. According to one former YouTube moderator, most people in this job hit a wall between three and five months. Moderators report that they feel desensitized from hours of watching explicit and violent videos and images. Others say that the job has made them paranoid in their daily lives, unable to trust others and suspecting the worst of the people they meet.

moderators in November 2014 in a Salon.com article.

Many companies use a two-tiered content moderation system. Basic moderation tasks are outsourced to places abroad, like the Philippines. More complex screening, which requires the moderator to be familiar with American culture, remains in the United States. After graduating from college, Rob took a contract job in Northern California as a content moderator in 2010. He moderated videos on YouTube. "I was pretty stoked," Rob said in an October 2014 interview that appeared on Wired.com. "It paid well, and I figured YouTube would look good on a résumé." For eight-hour shifts, Rob sat at a desk in YouTube's offices and reviewed batches of ten videos at a time. He deleted videos full of hate and gore: animal torture, street fights, suicide

Outsourced moderators perform basic moderation tasks from computer stations halfway around the world. Work that depends on cultural knowledge, typically remains in-house.

bombings, decapitations, and traffic accidents. Eventually, the constant exposure to these videos began to take a toll on him and he quit for another job a few months before his one-year contract expired.

TYPES OF MODERATION

There are several methods of website moderation that a moderator and site can follow. These include premoderation, postmoderation, reactive moderation, distributed moderation, and automated moderation. Sites and moderators evaluate each method to determine which best balances the community's need to share and engage and still protects users from offensive material.

Premoderation provides the highest level of control over the content displayed on a website. When a user submits a comment or image for publication on the site, it is placed in a queue for review. The site's moderator reviews each item in the queue before allowing it to be posted and visible on the website. Premoderation ensures that inappropriate and offensive content stays off a website. One of the downsides of this method is that it delays users from being able to see comments as they are being made. This can disrupt, slow, and eventually halt any conversation among users. In addition, premoderation can become more costly as a community grows and more moderators are needed to keep up with the volume of activity.

As an alternative, postmoderation allows all content to be displayed on a site as soon as a user submits it. At the same time, a copy of the comment is placed into a queue for the moderator to review. Upon review, the moderator can remove the post if necessary. While this method is faster than premoderation, it can also become costly and time consuming as communities grow, because every comment has to be reviewed.

Reactive moderation relies on community members to flag content that is inappropriate or offensive. Some communities use reactive moderation in addition to other methods, as a safety net. When members report inappropriate content, the moderator can review and remove it if needed.

Distributed moderation uses a rating system in which community members vote on whether comments are appropriate

Moderating websites is a flexible job. Often, moderators can set their own hours, allowing them time to meet friends during the day for a casual outing.

or violate the site's rules. Senior moderators guide the community members, who have control of comments or forum posts. This type of moderation is most often used within an organization, where several staff members can rate comments and determine if content should be allowed or reviewed.

In addition to relying on human moderators, some sites employ automated moderation systems. These systems use technical tools to process comments, by applying defined rules to approve or reject comments. For example, a site can use a word filter that has a list of banned words. The tool scans through submissions, removing any banned words or replacing them with an approved alternate. It may block or remove the message entirely.

A FLEXIBLE JOB

Website moderators rarely work at a company's physical office. Instead, most website moderators work remotely from anywhere in the world, as long as they have computers and internet access. Often, the hours are very flexible, making this job an ideal option for students or people with other commitments. People with a positive attitude, who love to interact with others online, may find this career very rewarding.

Chapter TWO

Education Requirements

Typically, there is no formal education requirement to become a website moderator. However, certain skills and experiences can improve a person's chances of landing a moderator job and performing well. Some website moderators may be required to edit photos and webpages, build software, and use existing moderation programs. They can learn these technologies through several paths, including formal classes, online workshops, or personal experience.

EDUCATIONAL CLASSES

While no formal degree is required for website moderators, people in this career must be familiar with the internet, how to navigate it, and how to make changes to websites. Therefore, courses in web design or even a web design degree can help students build the web skills that they need as a website moderator.

Understanding the internet and the world wide web and how to maneuver through websites, chat rooms, forums, and emerging social media are essential skills for website moderators.

Some adult and teen education programs provide classes for people interested in learning about web design and computer programming. Teens can enroll in single classes or a long-term program that involves several classes and leads to a certificate or degree. Students enrolled in these types of programs typically take classes that teach them how to use web software, such as Adobe Photoshop, Java, Macromedia Flash, and Ajax. Other useful classes teach design theory, web animation, and digital imaging. Students should also take classes to learn how to use HTML (hypertext markup language), the standard markup language used to create web pages.

Teens can also take online classes in web design and computer programming. Online educational organizations such as the Khan Academy and Lynda.com offer courses in a variety of subjects, including web design. With the Khan Academy, students can watch a series of short lectures on YouTube to learn how to use HTML and CSS to make webpages. The site's lectures are free to anyone around the world. Lynda.com is another online education company that offers thousands of video courses taught by industry experts. For a fee, students can take technology courses in topics such as web design and programming.

Using headphones and a laptop, a student watches a video for an online training course in web design to broaden her technical and online skills.

Some students choose to earn a degree in web development or design. Community colleges offer two-year associate's degrees in web design and development. Other students choose to pursue a bachelor's or master's degree at a college or university, studying web development and other technical topics. Courses in communications, media studies, writing, and ethics, as well as those on social media and online communications, are helpful for teens interested in moderating websites.

EXPERIENCE IN AN ONLINE COMMUNITY

Getting experience online, either as a volunteer moderator or a forum participant, is a good way to prepare for a job as a website moderator. For those who have never worked as a website moderator, one of the easiest ways to get a foot in the door and gain some experience is to volunteer to moderate a community or forum in which you are already involved. Some communities offer volunteer moderator positions to members who participate regularly and have the respect of other community members. Alternatively, some charity or nonprofit organizations accept volunteer, unpaid moderators. In addition to providing valuable on-the-job experience, volunteering gives teens an opportunity to network with other website moderators and industry professionals, which may lead to future job opportunities.

Sue, who works as an online community manager, recommends teens follow their interests and get involved online. In a January 2012 article that appeared on Sue on the Web, she advises those interested in working as website moderators to "get involved in online communities that deal with topics, or subjects, you are familiar with, or are interested in. Start sharing useful information—in other words make sure that each one of your posts and comments offers something of value to the community. Then as you become a valued member of the community offer your services to the community manager/admin as a volunteer moderator. Regardless of whether a position is paid or not, experience is experience, and by volunteering you will learn an immense amount of community management and moderation skills. Later when you are ready to move on and spread your wings I am sure the CM's/Admin's of the community will be happy to give you a reference that you can use when you apply for a paying position."

Even without working as a moderator, just being an active member of an online community can help a teen gain valuable experience. Moderators need to understand how the community or website that they want to moderate works. Simply participating in a community exposes teens to a wide range of member behaviors, both good and bad. Observing how moderators deal with different situations and people online and apply the site's guidelines can be a valuable learning experience for future moderators.

SOCIAL MEDIA AND ONLINE PUBLISHING KNOWLEDGE

Many moderators perform work for international companies, protecting their brand from inappropriate and libelous user-generated content. As users increasingly turn to social media to interact, having social media skills and being familiar with multiple platforms is becoming increasingly important for people who want to work as moderators. Understanding how to use and maneuver popular platforms—Facebook, Twitter, various photo sharing sites, blogs, and other online media—is a valuable skill for potential moderators. The best way to get this knowledge is to join these platforms and get active by liking, posting, pinning, commenting, and sharing.

A woman uses her smartphone to check social media updates. As the use of social media platforms increases, increased moderation and supervision of these sites will be needed.

In addition, some employers require that moderators have professional or personal experience in online publishing. Having a personal blog or website or managing one for an organization can show that a person has these experiences and skills.

SPECIALIZED KNOWLEDGE

Some of the biggest companies in the world have teams of moderators who work around the clock to protect their brand, reputation, and online communities. Their websites can have a very specific focus, from gaming sites to specialized sports sites. Teens who have hobbies, special skills, or interests that match a website's focus may be a good fit to moderate that site. For example, a person who is a photography buff may be a good choice to moderate an amateur photography forum, while a teen who enjoys baking may be a good fit for a cooking forum.

Behind the Screen with a Reddit Moderator

Reddit is an entertainment and news website where registered community members submit content, such as posts or links, making it like an online bulletin board. The site's content is divided into subcategories called subreddits, each of which has a moderator. Reddit moderator /u/noeatnosleep moderates more than 60 subreddits. He spends about 30 to 40 hours each week moderating. In an interview that appeared on www.marketersguidetoreddit.com, he discussed what he liked and disliked about moderating.

   Likes: "I only moderate communities I'm interested in. You'll notice a theme through my subs; sociopolitical discussion, motorcycles, and tech. As far as what I specifically enjoy about the job; I really enjoy being a gardener and cleaning out the bad weeds and bugs in subreddits that I'm passionate about. Getting rid of trolls and spam is a joy for me. When I'm finished for the day I can stand back and admire the clean and functioning subreddit, something a lot of people take for granted. I consider moderating a glorified janitor's job, and there is a unique pride that janitors have."

Dislikes: "I do automate a lot of what I don't like to do. I have various bots and scripts that work as traps and/or alarms in various situations. These are almost always tied to some sort of manual approval and verification. Most of these tools are home-made, but Reddit does supply a little of this."

The entertainment and news website Reddit functions as an online bulletin board for many registered community members.

Lisa Craven, the chief executive officer at Moderation Gateway, a company that offers training for online moderators, says that having specialized knowledge about a particular subject can give a moderator an advantage when applying for a job. "I've heard of many sites that require moderators who are an authority on a certain subject and would be very pleased to find you. If you have extensive experience of online games, for example by being a player, don't discount this knowledge as it is very valuable. Having player perspective will give you added insight when it comes to performing moderation tasks," she wrote in a November 2014 article on the Real Ways to Earn Money site.

FOREIGN LANGUAGE SKILLS

The internet is global, with people from different countries, backgrounds, and languages participating. For example, users from Spain, Egypt, and the United States can engage in a conversation on a message board about gaming. International companies offer message boards and forums to customers in many countries, often

A student studies a foreign language with her teacher. As the internet reaches people around the world, knowing one or more foreign languages is a useful skill for website moderators.

in several languages. In addition, social media agencies provide moderation services in more than 50 languages. As a result, moderators who are fluent in one or more foreign languages are often in demand. In addition to having a command of the traditional language, knowing the language's contemporary slang phrases and words is important, as these words often appear in online comments.

TRAINING

As the need for website moderation has grown, some companies offer training for moderators. Some training is in-house, where companies hire and train moderators for the specific duties required for their forums and platforms. Other companies have designed moderation training programs or classes that anyone can sign up to take.

In 2013, training company Moderation Gateway introduced the first certified training course for user-generated content moderation. The training is designed to set new standards for best practices in moderation. The course prepares students with the skills and confidence needed to become successful online moderators. The self-paced course includes audio and video modules focusing on different types of moderation, related legislation, best practices, and child safety issues online. It also includes an online glossary, links for further reading, and a forum for past and present students to ask and answer questions. Upon completing the training course, moderators earn a professional certification. Moderation Gateway developed the course in partnership with eModeration, a social media management company that offers online moderation services. "Moderators have a really important role to play in keeping sites safe and appropriate. I passionately believe that only experienced, trained people should moderate online content, particularly where issues like child safety are involved. Certification means that brands can be sure they're getting high-quality, trained moderators working on their behalf," said Tamara Littleton, eModeration's CEO, in a June 2013 press release about the training.

Melanie Burnside is an experienced moderator and community manager who works for eModeration. Burnside has moderated websites and social media for a variety of clients, including LEGO and MTV. Although she was already an experienced moderator, she decided to take Moderation Gateway's training course to validate her current skills and earn a professional certification. She says that she liked how the course was self-paced, which allowed her to work through the modules on her own timetable. In her opinion, having a library of relevant research and resources in one place is one of the most useful parts of the course. She says that it provides a quick and easy way for beginning and experienced moderators to keep informed on changes in industry regulations, legislation, and platforms. Although she mainly moderates content for adult users, Burnside appreciated the child protection module, saying that it made her aware of how children and young adults can be subtly manipulated online.

While there is no specific education required to be a website moderator, there are several ways that teens can prepare themselves for this job. Taking classes to improve web and technical skills and getting experience online and on social media will help a teen build the skills needed to moderate websites. Participating in moderator training, either through online courses or company training, can also build a teen's portfolio of skills that will help him or her be a successful website moderator.

Chapter THREE

Helpful Skills

Moderating a website can be a tricky task. It requires a mix of technical skills, impeccable judgment, and spot-on intuition. Not everyone who applies to be a moderator has the skills needed to be successful. Yet take a look at some of the most active and engaging forums on the internet, and there will probably be a skilled moderator driving the site.

TECHNICAL SKILLS

Website moderators are expected to have a variety of technical skills. They should be comfortable with computers, the internet, and using social media. The technical skills required can vary by moderation job but can include knowledge of programming languages such as HTML, graphic design, and animation. They should also be comfortable using Microsoft Office Suite programs such as Word, Excel, and PowerPoint.

Moderators should also have a working knowledge and understanding of various community platforms. They should know how to maneuver forums, post blogs, upload photos, and

From a computer in his office, a moderator edits photos that will be placed on a website. Every day, he uses a variety of computer and technical skills on the job.

work with user comments. As the guardian of forum content, moderators need to be able to move, merge, add, and delete text, links, and graphics. They will be expected to assist users with technical problems when posting or accessing the site. Moderators are also expected to move discussion threads to the appropriate sections of the forum, close or lock threads when activity in them declines, and edit posts. Sometimes, they will temporarily or permanently delete entire threads of comments.

HTML: The Web's Language

Website moderators should know how to use HTML, the language of the World Wide Web. "HTML" stands for "HyperText Markup Language." Developed by scientist Tim Berners-Lee in 1990, it is the language used to create web pages that can be displayed in a web browser. As the internet has grown, HTML has also been modified and improved every few years.

Every web page on the internet is written in HTML. HTML is like the skeleton that gives a web page its structure. HTML uses tags to mark blocks of text on a page. HTML tags are keywords surrounded by angle brackets. They separate normal text from HTML code. Different tags perform different functions. Simple tags give instructions for text formatting. For example, <strong> is a tag. It is used to mark text that should be bold. Tags normally come in pairs. The first tag is the start tag, while the second tag is the end tag. The end tag has a slash before the

A computer displays HTML code, the programming language of the world wide web. This code creates the web pages shown when a person browses the internet.

tag name. For example, **this is bold text**.
The text for a website is viewed through a web browser like Internet Explorer or Google Chrome. The web browser reads the HTML file and translates it into a visible web page. The browser does not show the tags on the page. Instead, the tags tell the web browser how to display the website's text or graphics.

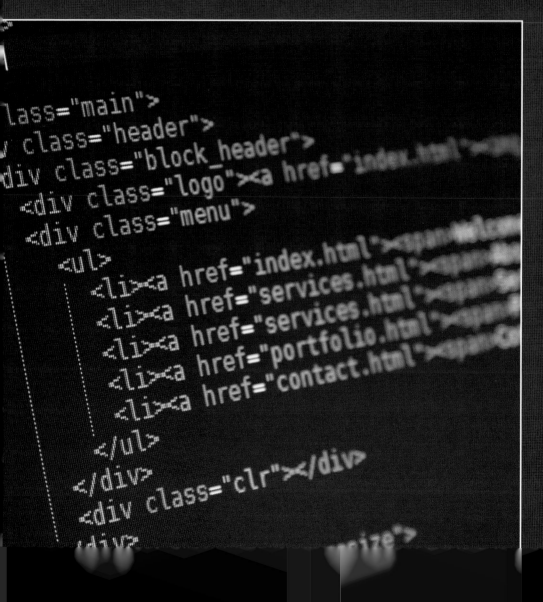

Because more content is moving to social media, moderators should have an excellent understanding of and ability to interact on various social media platforms. And perhaps most importantly, website moderators should have the ability to learn new technical skills quickly. As technology changes rapidly, moderators who can keep up with changes and master new skills quickly have the best chance to be successful.

COMMUNICATION SKILLS

On a daily basis, website moderators and online community managers communicate with users, website owners, coworkers, and employers. In order to be successful, people in this job should have strong written

At Google offices around the world, a variety of internet professionals must be able to work together and communicate clearly and effectively with coworkers and customers.

and verbal communication skills. They should be well spoken and able to communicate their thoughts into words effectively.

In some cases, moderators join in a forum conversation. They encourage others to participate and add expert comments. In some cases, moderators will pose as a user to steer a conversation in a particular direction or offer advice. To be effective, they must be able to send clear messages to users and post engaging content that encourages participation in an online community.

Website moderators also communicate with clients and coworkers. In these messages, they must use effective language, with proper grammar and spelling. Messages should be of an appropriate length and subject. According to Google DC Community Manager Corrie Davidson, website moderators should be able to communicate effectively in a variety of ways to several different audiences. "Whether it be short form or long form, you have to be able to write," she said in a January 2013 interview that appeared on Mashable. "Blog posts, guest articles, emails, proposals, social content—you have to be able to craft your ideas and messages to fit any medium."

In addition, Davidson says that website moderators and community managers must also be friendly and approachable, both online and offline. "They need to be outgoing, friendly and relatable. They should be comfortable interacting with people offline as well as online; a natural networker," she said.

IMPARTIALITY AND GOOD JUDGMENT

Website moderators are often faced with making difficult decisions. Should they remove a post or let it remain? Should they ban a user or give him or her a warning? When should they intervene in a thread that is getting increasingly heated or off topic? How should moderators enforce the website's guidelines? Making these difficult decisions requires good judgment. The decisions that moderators make affect the entire community. Many moderators will delete comments that they disagree with or ban members they think are spamming. Yet this can be a mistake. If their posts are deleted without explanation, members may feel alienated and angry. And if a moderator's decisions appear to be too heavy-handed, forum members may leave the group because they feel that they are not being allowed to express their opinions.

Moderators should always be impartial. Many times, discussions can become heated. A moderator cannot let his or her personal views on an issue affect the decisions he or she makes moderating the site. For example, a moderator who supports a local candidate for mayor should not remove all posts that criticize the candidate as long as the posts follow the rules of the website. In some situations, users may post insulting comments about a moderator or another user. No matter the insult, the moderator must keep a level head and respond appropriately to the offending user. A moderator's response should calm the situation, not aggravate it.

Many successful moderators say that they edit member posts or delete accounts only as a last resort. Instead, they try to resolve the dispute by contacting the member first and explaining the rule they have broken. The moderator can then ask the member to remove or edit the post themselves. In this way, the member understands the actions of the moderator and feels as if he or she is still a valued member of the online community.

UNDERSTANDING THE AUDIENCE

In order to engage community members and encourage active and vibrant discussions, website moderators should have a good knowledge of the site's users. Knowing what type of people they are, how they interact, and what they care about can help a moderator be more effective and empathetic. "You're dealing with a bunch of different personalities. If you're not empathetic, you're never going to be able to put yourself in those people's shoes, which means you won't be able to communicate a message to them," said Tim McDonald, the community manager for HuffPost Live in a January 2013 interview that appeared on Mashable.

For many websites, a good moderator gives the site's users a voice. Users feel that they have a place to ask questions and express their opinions. A good moderator, who understands his or her audience, creates an environment in which people feel like they are part of a conversation. At HuffPost Live, Tim McDonald says that he aims to turn single comments from users into a back-and-forth conversation among users. He says that about 70 percent of the site's comments are made in response to other user's comments.

DEDICATION AND MOTIVATION

Website moderators often work by themselves, at home. At home, they are surrounded by countless distractions, such as kids, pets, chores, and even the television. In order to be successful, website moderators need to be able to put aside these distractions and focus on moderating tasks. Often, they sit for long periods of time, staring at a computer screen and reading

Some website moderators choose to work late night or early morning hours because it better fits their schedule and lifestyle than a traditional nine to five job

messages until a user needs their help. Without a manager on site to look over their shoulders and make sure that they are doing their work, moderators must motivate themselves to get the job done.

The work hours for a moderator can vary from job to job. Unlike traditional nine to five jobs, moderators can usually work at any time of day or night. They can be called upon to resolve a situation at all hours. They are often working during peak activity times, on weekends, nights, and holidays, when many people are online and posting.

ORGANIZED AND DETAILED

Moderators should be organized and have a good eye for detail. Some moderators work for different sites and forums. They manage multiple platforms, track site use and feedback, and compile this information for site owners and employers. Being organized is an essential skill in order to keep up with these varied responsibilities. Website moderators often need to juggle multiple tasks at once. Being organized is one way to ensure they do not drop the ball on anything that is asked of them.

Every day, website moderators review thousands of comments and posts. Successful moderators have an eye for detail and pick out an issue from thousands of harmless comments. They can read between the lines of a forum conversation and recognize what is really being said, whether it be a veiled threat or a coded reference to drug use. Then, moderators can resolve the issue according to the website's guidelines.

Chapter FOUR

Finding a Job as a Website Moderator

F or people who like to work with computers and interact with others online, a job as a website moderator may be a good fit. The growing popularity of forums and websites has sparked the need for moderators. Companies that want to launch a forum, but do not have someone to moderate it, are looking to hire moderators. Some want moderators to simply delete spam, profanity, and other offensive content.

Without the work of website moderators to clean up websites, chat rooms and forums, a person surfing the internet might unintentionally come across offensive content.

Some companies want moderators to build an online community by participating in it.

VOLUNTEER FOR EXPERIENCE

To get started in this career, many people volunteer for nonpaying moderator positions. All they need is a computer with a high-speed internet connection. In these roles, they gain valuable experience moderating a community. They learn the tricks of the trade, including how to encourage community growth and deal with problem users. Having experience, even unpaid, makes a person a more attractive candidate for a paid position. Once you have some experience, you may be ready to turn a hobby into a paying position.

Not all websites work the same way. The way to becoming a moderator for one site may be different from the path for another site. Each community functions in its own way, and this includes how they pick their moderators. Some sites select moderators without a formal application process. Other sites invite interested candidates to apply.

LOOK IN CURRENT FORUMS

Sometimes, the easiest place to find a job as a website moderator is to look in communities where a person is already actively involved. Community members are familiar with the style, content, and rules of a forum or website. Active users are often well known among other community members. Their posts encourage others to participate in a conversation. By participating regularly, members can show that they are knowledgeable, helpful, and fair, all of which are qualities of a good moderator. In

A job applicant shakes hands with an interviewer and gives him her resume. Presenting a professional image during an interview shows an applicant is serious about the position.

addition, members can show through their actions on a site that they understand the site's rules, have good judgment, and are trustworthy. If they gain the respect of others in the community through frequent, thoughtful interactions, they will be at the top of the applicant list when a moderator job opens. Those in charge of a website might even notice a member's positive contributions and invite them to become a moderator when a position is available.

Members interested in moderating should ask current forum administrators if there are any open positions. They can send an email or private message to the current administrator and let them know that they are interested if any opportunities arise. Other times, the website might advertise that moderators are needed and for interested candidates to contact them.

David Sutton-Rowe is the moderator of the Spain forum on ExpatFocus.com. After moving to Spain from the United Kingdom, he discovered ExpatFocus.com. He became an active member on its forum. "When we got to Spain, we had to wait 18 months for a telephone and ADSL to be installed, it was then I decided to join Expat Focus and write about the things I knew in getting established here in Spain. After a little while I was asked if I wanted to be a forum moderator. It didn't take me long to make up my mind, I looked upon it as a learning experience where I could help others moving to or living here in Spain and also learn new things myself. I feel really good when I can help someone with something I have personal knowledge or experience of and I'm very happy to direct people to other sources of information if I can't assist directly. I have had some wonderful things said to me by members of the forums which makes the task of moderating feel very worthwhile. If I'm able to help anyone in the forums I will do so!" he said in a November 2015 interview that appeared on ExpatFocus.com.

ONLINE JOB BOARDS

Many companies looking to hire moderators post open positions on online job boards, such as Monster.com, Indeed.com, or SimplyHired.com. Candidates can search these sites for open positions. Examples of position titles to search for include "forum administrator," "forum moderator," "website moderator," and "forum leader." Some jobs can also be found using broad search

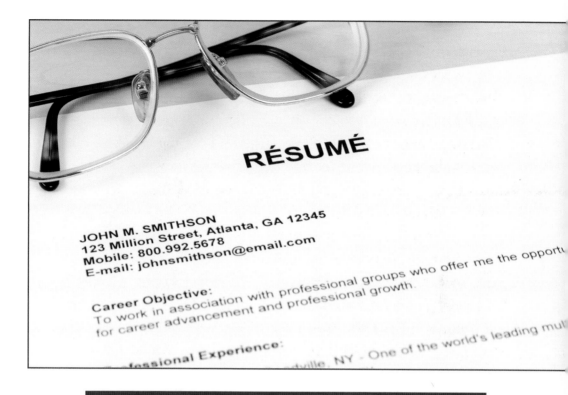

RÉSUMÉ

JOHN M. SMITHSON
123 Million Street, Atlanta, GA 12345
Mobile: 800.992.5678
E-mail: johnsmithson@email.com

Career Objective:
To work in association with professional groups who offer me the opport
for career advancement and professional growth.

...ssional Experience: ...ville, NY - One of the world's leading mul

Candidates search online job boards for open website moderation jobs. When a position is posted, applicants can send in a resume that lists their qualifications for the job.

engines such as Bing, Google, or Yahoo and searching for online forum administrator jobs. Once a position is found, a person can read the descriptions of the position and company to learn what qualifications are required. The postings also provide instruction on how to apply for the position.

MODERATION COMPANIES

As forums and message boards have exploded in popularity online, many companies do not have the expertise or desire to moderate their websites themselves. To fill this need, professional website moderation companies have emerged to handle the moderation duties for client websites. These companies hire many people to work as moderators. In these jobs, moderators can work for a variety of different websites and clients. Companies like eModeration, ICUC, Mod Squad, and Lithium frequently hire website moderators.

NETWORKING

Some people find jobs as website moderators by keeping their eyes and ears open. They find leads to open positions on social media, through tweets or other posts. They network with administrators of other forums. Sometimes, a forum may not have a job opening, but the administrator can refer a person to companies, websites, or other forums that may be hiring moderators or forum administrators.

ADVANCEMENT

After a person has landed a job moderating a website, they typically have several basic responsibilities. They monitor a forum or chat room, remove posts that are offensive or off topic, and enforce the site's rules. Over time, experienced moderators may be assigned additional responsibilities.

Very active websites and chat rooms often have more than one moderator. There is a hierarchy of moderators that work together, including staff moderators, senior moderators, and website or forum administrators. Staff moderators who demonstrate a high level of skill may be promoted to become senior moderators.

Senior moderators often have additional responsibilities. They may be asked to supervise a team of staff moderators.

Working for ICUC

For people who enjoy participating in forums and experimenting with social media, a moderator job with ICUC may be just the thing. Founded in 2002, ICUC Moderation Services, Inc. (ICUC) is a Canadian company that focuses on protecting brands. They hire a team of skilled moderators, many of whom work from home, to monitor and protect their clients' information and content. ICUC offers services in more than ten languages to clients around the world, 24 hours a day.

As a home moderation expert at ICUC, a moderator may work with clients such as Chevron, Starbucks, Virgin Mobile, and ProBass Fishing. They are responsible for helping to promote the client's brand on social networks. They also secure online promotions, often through social media. ICUC home moderators moderate a variety of forums 24 hours a day, including weekends and holidays. They delete and approve comments and remind users of the forum's rules as needed. They work for a wide variety of clients, including government agencies, private companies, entertainment and media companies, and nonprofit organizations. Moderators generally work eight-hour shifts and can be part-time or full-time, depending on the team's needs. Once hired, ICUC trains its moderators for their specific job responsibilities.

Senior moderators may also be very involved in hiring new staff moderators. When there is a job opening, they interview potential candidates over email, chat, or Skype. They review the candidate's history and experience and give their input as to whether or not the candidate should be hired. Once a new moderator joins the team, senior moderators are often responsible for training the new hire for his or her specific assignment, teaching technical skills as well as website policies. Senior moderators may also take on more responsibility for making the website's rules. They can be involved in creating, writing, and editing guidelines, policies, and procedures for the website that they monitor.

FREELANCE MODERATORS

Rather than working for a company, some people decide to work as freelance moderators. Freelance moderators offer

A freelance website moderator consults with a client on his cell phone. Building a good relationship with clients can help a freelance moderator get referrals for new work and clients.

their services to employers without a long-term commitment to them. As a freelancer, they are free to work for a variety of clients, taking on as many or as few as they want. They often charge by the hour, day, or job.

The key to being a successful freelance moderator is finding work. Freelancers have to look constantly for new jobs to replace completed ones. Searching forums and job boards and networking with contacts can lead to finding freelance work. Each successful job builds up the freelancer's résumé and can lead to repeat work. Freelancers can also use satisfied clients as referrals to get future jobs.

Those who are considering a freelance career should seek out the advice of an industry mentor. A mentor is someone who is willing to spend his or her time sharing expertise and guiding another person on his or her career development. Mentors have worked in website moderation or administration. Relying on their experience, they can answer questions and give advice to freelance moderators who are beginning their own careers.

MODERATORS WANTED

With so many active user communities online, website moderators are needed around the internet. People working in these jobs operate behind the scenes to help users resolve issues, make sure a site's rules are being followed, and encourage a vibrant online community. For teens who enjoy being online, demonstrating their interest, experience, and skill with online communities may lead to a job as a website moderator.

Chapter FIVE

Future Career Growth

As e-commerce continues to expand, companies are realizing the importance of having an internet presence on many different platforms and social media outlets. As the internet becomes more integrated in daily life, the need for website moderators is expected to be strong. According to the Bureau of Labor Statistics, employment of web developers is projected to grow 27 percent from 2014 to 2024, a rate that is much faster than the average for all occupations. As more websites and forums go active online, moderators will be needed to oversee them.

The increase in mobile device use is one factor driving job growth for web careers. Specialized websites will be created that work on mobile devices with many different screen sizes, including smartphones and tablets. As the number of websites increases,

As companies design and develop new mobile internet devices, people will have new ways to go online at any time, from anywhere in the world.

there will be more opportunities for website moderators. Website moderators with experience using multiple programming languages and multimedia tools, such as Flash and Photoshop, will have the best opportunities.

Although website moderation can be done from anywhere in the world, some moderation jobs may be moved to countries with lower wages, which will decrease job growth in the United States. However, the work of a website moderator often relies on a knowledge of cultural nuances in order to interact and communicate effectively with users. This favors the hiring of American moderators and limits the ability of this job to be moved to workers in other countries.

Moderating Algorithm

Algorithmia, a company that works with algorithms, hopes to use one of its programs to moderate websites in the future. An algorithm is a set of steps to complete a task. A computer algorithm uses specific tasks or processes that need to be completed in a specific order. In 2015, Algorithmia introduced a new algorithm to find nudity in pictures. Users submit a photo on the company's website (isitnude.com) and the algorithm reviews the image and determines if there is any nudity in it. The company developed the algorithm for a client who wanted to be able to screen images for a kid-friendly website and make sure they were not pornographic. Kenny Daniel, the company's chief technical officer, says that the company took some existing image recognition software and combined it to create the naked-identifying code. "We'd done quite a bit of work on image recognition," Daniel said in a June 2015 interview that appeared on Wired. com. "One of our engineers took some algorithms off the shelf, things like image detection, skin color detection, and then put them together."

The company admits that the current version of the algorithm is raw and needs to be refined. At present, it cannot recognize individual body parts. In addition, innocent beach photos might get flagged. And because it uses skin tone to identify nakedness, the algorithm does not work on black and white photos. Yet even with its current limits, Algorithmia's ultimate goal is to develop a system that can operate without human help.

RELATED CAREER: WEBSITE DEVELOPER

People who work as website moderators can use their existing skill set as a base to move into several related careers. Almost every company and organization today has a website. Customers visit a company's website to learn more about products, find store locations, and buy products online. Designing a website

A website developer works at his computer to build a new and engaging website for a client. Some website moderators also perform web development work.

that is creative and attractive to customers is the job of web developers. A website developer creates the layout, color scheme, and general design of a website. He or she creates specialized, eye-catching websites for a variety of clients. Because every organization is different, web developers work with each client to create an individual design that appeals to customers. After the site is built, they regularly adjust and add updates to the site. In some cases, web developers also create content for the website. They are also responsible for the site's technical aspects, including its performance (speed) and capacity (traffic). They might work for a company or organization directly. They might also be hired independently.

Some web developers build an entire website from start to finish. Others specialize in a particular area of web development. Back-end web developers work on the technical construction of the site. They create the site's framework and make sure that it works as designed. They also add procedures for others to add pages and content in the future. Front-end developers focus on a website's appearance. They design the layout, integrate graphics, and other content. Once a website is live, webmasters maintain and update the sites. They monitor the site to make sure everything is working properly and respond to user comments and questions.

Website moderators who know how to use HTML, Adobe Photoshop, Java, Macromedia Flash, and other web software and have taken classes in web design or development will have opportunities to work in web development. In addition, the communication skills learned as a website moderator will be needed as a web developer to deal effectively with clients.

SOCIAL MEDIA MANAGER

Social media is quickly becoming an important platform for companies to interact with customers. On Twitter, Facebook, and Instagram, customers discuss companies and their brands. Loyal customers can become advocates for a company. On the flip side, an unsatisfied customer can tweet to the world about his or her negative experience with the company. Companies are also learning about what their customers want, building relationships, and getting ideas for product improvement through social media.

As social media increases in popularity and more platforms are introduced, social media managers will be needed to monitor and maintain a company's presence on social media. For people with website moderating experience and skills, the jump to becoming a social media manager should be an easy one.

Social media managers are responsible for promoting and protecting a company's brand on social media. In this role, they create content such as tweets, pictures posted on Instagram, or a Pinterest board of company products. They also respond to customer comments and answer questions. Most of the time, a social media manager deals with people who already have a relationship with a company and its products or at least have heard of the brand.

Brit Thompson is a social media manager at Sprout Social, a social media management company. She spends her day interacting with her clients' customers, making sure that they have a positive experience with the brands. In a typical day, she responds to and helps customers, writes or creates social media

content, analyzes her clients' social media performance, and meets with her team to talk about strategy and next steps. Many of these tasks are similar to those performed by website moderators, making them easily able to transition to this type of job in the future.

COMMUNITY MANAGER

Website moderators are also well suited to move into the related career of community management. Fueled by the rise in social media, community managers advocate for a company and its brand on social networks. Creating a social persona, they go online and actively interact with the online community. They work to connect with potential customers

A social media manager responds to a customer comment on her tablet. She answers customer questions and creates content to post on the company's social media sites.

and spread the word about the company, its brand, and products. Most of the time, community managers are targeting people who know very little about the brand they represent. They aim to engage new users and raise awareness about the company and its brand in order to grow the brand's community.

Sarah Nagel is a community manager at Spout Social. In a typical day, she attends Twitter chats as "Sprout Sarah" and moderates a Sprout chat room. She researches ways to connect with new people and spread the word about her clients' brand. She blogs on external sites. She also reviews analytics to determine which social media efforts are yielding the most traffic.

A community manager works online to moderate a chat room and connect with new customers. With each online interaction, she increases awareness about her company's brand and products.

As the internet continues to grow, the future looks bright for web careers, including website moderators. Without guidance, the web's forums and chat rooms can turn into chaotic environments. As long as these spaces exist, there will be a need for moderators to keep them in line. For teens who are active in online communities and social media, a career as a website moderator can be a great way to make money doing something they enjoy.

Glossary

algorithm A procedure or formula for solving a problem.

analyze To study something carefully and methodically.

automated Using machines instead of people to complete a job or task.

bigotry Intolerance toward those who hold different opinions from oneself.

e-commerce Selling of products and services over the internet.

empathetic Recognizing and sharing another person's feelings.

engage To attract, occupy, or hold someone's interest or attention.

filtering A process that removes unwanted material.

freelance Referring to a person who is self-employed and not committed to a particular employer for a long period.

graphics An image or a series of images shown on a website.

impartial Not biased and treating all equally.

liability The state of being legally responsible for something.

libelous An untrue statement that causes people to think poorly of someone.

mentor A more experienced person who guides and teaches a less experienced person.

metrics Measurements used to track and assess the status of a business process.

moderator A person who oversees an internet forum or chat room.

network To interact with people to exchange information and make contacts in order to further one's career.

nuances The subtle differences in meaning, expression, or sound.

offensive Causing someone to feel angry, hurt, or upset.

profane Something that is obscene or goes against religious teachings.

résumé A detailed document used by a job seeker to present his or her work background and skills.

social media Tools that allow people, companies, and organizations to create and share information through the internet.

For More Information

Bureau of Labor Statistics
Postal Square Building
2 Massachusetts Avenue, NE
Washington, DC 20212-0001
(202) 691-5200
Website: www.bls.gov

The Bureau of Labor Statistics of the US Department of Labor
is the principal federal agency responsible for measuring
labor market activity, working conditions, and price changes
in the economy. It collects, analyzes, and disseminates
essential economic information to support public and
private decision making, including forecasts about future
career growth.

Canada's Association of Information Technology Professionals
(CIPS)
National Office
5090 Explorer Drive, Suite 801
Mississauga, Ontario L4W 4T9
(905) 602-1370
Website: www.cips.ca

CIPS is a professional organization for information technology
professionals in Canada, representing more than 6,000 IT
professionals on important issues affecting the IT industry.

41 East 11th Street
New York, NY 10003
(646) 661-0477
Website: www.emoderation.com

Emoderation delivers multilingual community management and
user-generated content moderation services, social media
consultancy, social listening, and social media crisis
management to clients in a wide range of industry sectors.

International Web Association (IWA)
119 E. Union Street Suite #A
Pasadena, CA 91103
(626) 449-3709
Website: http://iwanet.org/

IWA is the industry's recognized leader in providing educational
and certification standards for web professionals. The
association supports more than 300,000 individual members
in 106 countries.

Society of Internet Professionals (SIP)
120 Carlton Street
Suite 305
Toronto, ON, M5A 4K2
(416) 891-4937
Website: www.sipgroup.org

SIP is an international nonprofit organization that strives to
enhance the educational and professional standards for
internet professionals.

Web Professionals
PO Box 584
Washington, IL 61571-0584
(916) 989-2933
Website: http://webprofessionals.org

WebProfessionals.org is a nonprofit association dedicated to
the support of people and organizations who create,
manage, or market websites. It provides education and
training resources as well as certification for those who work
in web careers.

WEBSITES

Because of the changing nature of internet links, Rosen Publishing
has developed an online list of websites related to the subject of
this book. This site is updated regularly. Please use this link to
access this list: http://www.rosenlinks.com/TTHIC/moder

For Further Reading

Bacon, Jono. *The Art of Community: Building the New Age of Participation*. Sebastopol, CA: O'Reilly Media, 2012.

Boyd, Danah. *It's Complicated: The Social Lives of Networked Teens*. New Haven, CT: Yale University Press, 2014.

Cooper, Nate, and Kim Gee. *Build Your Own Website: A Comic Guide to HTML, CSS, and WordPress*. San Francisco, CA: No Starch Press, 2014.

Endsley, Kezia. *Website Design*. New York, NY: Cavendish Square Publishing, 2015.

Gray, Leon. *What Is a Blog and How Do I Use It?* New York, NY: Rosen Educational Services, 2014.

Greek, Joe. *Social Network-Powered Information Sharing*. New York: NY: Rosen Publishing, 2014.

Howe, Shay. *Learn to Code HTML and CSS: Develop and Style Websites*. San Francisco, CA: New Riders, 2014.

Hunter, Nick. *Social Networking: Big Business on Your Computer*. New York, NY: Gareth Stevens, 2012.

Klein, Rebecca T. *Career Building Through Using Digital Publishing Tools*. New York, NY: Rosen Publishing, 2014.

La Bella, Laura. *Careers in Web Development*. New York, NY: Rosen Publishing, 2011.

Lopuck, Lisa. *Web Design for Dummies. 3rd ed.* Hoboken, NJ: Wiley, 2012.

Lusted, Marcia Amidon. *Career Building Through Using Multimedia Art and Animation Tools*. New York, NY: Rosen Publishing, 2014.

Martin, Chris. *Build Your Own Web Site*. New York, NY: Rosen Publishing, 2014.

Ng, Deborah. *Online Community Management for Dummies*. Hoboken, NJ: Wiley, 2011.

Robbins, Jennifer Niederst. *Learning Web Design: A Beginner's Guide to HTML, CSS, JavaScript, and Web Graphics. 4th ed.* Sebastopol, CA: O'Reilly Media, 2012.

Staley, Erin. *Career Building Through Creating Mobile Apps*. New York, NY: Rosen Publishing, 2014.

Suen, Anastasia. *Career Building Through Using Search Engine Optimization Techniques*. New York, NY: Rosen Publishing, 2014.

Wilkinson, Colin. *Going Live: Launching Your Digital Business*. New York, NY: Rosen Publishing, 2012.

Willett, Edward. *Career Building Through Using Digital Design Tools*. New York, NY: Rosen Publishing, 2014.

Wooster, Patricia. *Flickr Cofounder and Web Community Creator Caterina Fake*. Minneapolis, MN: Lerner, 2014.

Bibliography

Barrett, Brian. "This Algorithm Wants to Find Who's Naked on the Internet." Wired.com, June 24, 2015. http://www.wired.com/2015/06/nude-recognition-algorithmia/.

Bureau of Labor Statistics. www.bls.org (accessed March 29, 2016).

Craven, Lisa. "How to Become a User-Generated Content Online Moderator." Real Ways to Earn, November 30, 2014. http://realwaystoearnmoneyonline.com/2014/07/how-to-become-a-user-generated-content-ugc-online-moderator.html.

Emoderation.com. http://www.emoderation.com/. (accessed March 29, 2016).

Emoderation. "Moderation Gateway launches first professional moderation training course." June 18, 2013. http://www.emoderation.com/moderation-gateway-launches-first-professional-moderation-training-course/.

Expat Articles. "Interview With David M Sutton-Rowe, Moderator - Spain Forum." Expat Focus, November 24, 2015. http://www.expatfocus.com/c/mode=prnt/id=2488/articles/spain/interview-with-david-m-sutton-rowe-moderator---spain-forum/.

Fredman, Josh. "How to Become a Website Moderator," *Houston Chronicle*. http://smallbusiness.chron.com/become-website-moderator-46570.html. (accessed April 1, 2016).

ICUC. http://icuc.social/. (accessed April 1, 2016).

Isquith, Elias. "'The Police of the Internet': Why the Human Costs of Social Media Are Greater Than You Think." Salon.com, November 4, 2014. http://www.salon.com/2014/11/04/the_police_of_the_internet_why_the_human_costs_of_social_media_are_greater_than_you_think/.

Knerl, Linsey. "How to Make Money as a Chat or Forum Moderator." Wisebread.com, April 21, 2015. http://www.wisebread.com/how-to-make-money-as-a-chat-or-forum-moderator.

Live World. http://www.liveworld.com/. (accessed March 30, 2016).

Lytle, Ryan. "10 Qualities of an Effective Community Manager," Mashable.com, January 27, 2013. http://mashable.com/2013/01/27/community-manager-qualities/#4xM6EwgY7Pqn.

Marketers Guide to Reddit. "The Mind of a Mod—An Interview with a Reddit Moderator." http://marketersguidetoreddit.com/interview-with-reddit-moderator-unoeatnosleep/. (accessed March 30, 2016).

Open Access Offshoring Blog. "What Are the Different Types of Content Moderation," Open Access, October 8, 2014. https://www.openaccessbpo.com/blog/different-types-content-moderation/.

Ruiz, Rebecca. "When Your Job Is To Moderate the Internet's Nastiest Trolls." Mashable.com, September 28, 2014. http://mashable.com/2014/09/28/moderating-the-trolls/#hluGLVNC7kql.

Snowden, Graham. "A Working Life: A Website Moderator." *Guardian*, February 3, 2012. http://www.theguardian.com/money/2012/feb/03/a-working-life-website-moderator.

Stone, Brad. "Policing the Web's Lurid Precincts." *New York Times*, July 18, 2010. http://www.nytimes.com/2010/07/19/technology/19screen.html?_r=3&mtrref=undefined&gwh=E2FCCC8B81BA10E7A4545B55E8812DBD&gwt=pay.

Sue on the Web. "How To Get Started As An Online Community Manager." January 25, 2012. http://sueontheweb.com/2012/01/how-to-get-started-as-an-online-community-manager.html.

Index

ABOUT THE AUTHOR

Carla Mooney is a graduate of the University of Pennsylvania. She writes for young people and is the author of numerous educational books. She enjoys using technology and is a member of several writing forums online.

PHOTO CREDITS

Designer: Nicole Russo; Editor: Bethany Bryan;
Photo Researcher: Bethany Bryan